Red Ear Slider Turtles

A Red Ear Slider Turtle Owner's Guide

Red Ear Slider Turtle care, where to buy, types, behavior, cost, handling, husbandry, diet, and much more included!

By Lolly Brown

Foreword

One of the three subspecies of the Pond Slider, the Red Ear Slider (RES) Turtle is not only popular in the United States; it has also gained great popularity around the world.

In the US, the normal range of occurrence for this sort of turtle is from Illinois to the Gulf of Mexico and from the East Coast to western Texas. This turtle likes to spend time in or around small bodies of slow moving water as well as ponds and marshes which is perfect for basking as well as providing abundance of food.

If you have ever considered keeping a Red Ear Slider Turtle for a pet, then this book is for you. This book contains information about everything you need to know regarding where to buy a Red Ear Slider Turtle, its behavior, its cost, how to handling and deal with it, husbandry, diet, and so much more. This little creature will keep you company for long time!

Table of Contents

Introduction

The Red Ear Slider Turtle (Trachemys scripta elegans), also called the Red Eared Terrapin, is a semiaquatic turtle that belongs to the Emydidae family. This turtle is one of the three subspecies of the Pond Slider.

The Red Ear Slider (RES) Turtle is not only popular in the United States. It has also gained great popularity worldwide as well. It could be because of its almost comical look as it bobs its head as if in agreement to some secret thought you had, or perhaps it's popularity comes from how the Red Eared Slider teaches its hobbyist/caregiver, by example, of how to enjoy life as it unfolds, to live in the moment and to appreciate the simple pleasures life has to offer - as it basks and soaks up rays.

They may seem shy at the onset of a new relationship - choosing to hide and shy away from company at the beginning - but once the Red Eared Slider turtle gets used to its new surroundings, once it gets to know the nooks and crannies of its new habitat and has properly surveyed its new digs, it will warm up to its new caregiver's presence.

Whatever it is and all in between, the Red Ear Slider Turtle has become the most frequently traded turtle the world over.

Glossary of Red Eared Slider Turtle Terms

Abscess – Refer to ear abscess.

Acrylic Aquarium – An alternative to the more common glass aquarium. They are lighter than an equivalent glass aquarium but are prone to scratching.

Aggression – RES are considered to be more aggressive than other similar turtles. They can easily compete out other turtles and male RES may harass females.

Alkaline – A pH level greater than 7. It is often contrasted with acid and has a greater concentration of hydroxyl ions.

Ammonia – A colorless compound of nitrogen and hydrogen. It is corrosive, toxic and may have an unpleasant odor. Waste and proteins in discarded food are key contributors to the presence of ammonia in tank water and toxicity can build within your tank if these levels go unchecked.

Anapsid – A group of amniotes, a microphylum of tetrapod vertebrates that include Sauropsida. The only members still in existence are the Testudines - turtles, tortoises, and terrapins.

Bacteria – A group of microorganisms that are widely distributed in our environment and in the tissues of plants and animals. RES keepers should be aware of beneficial, harmful and infectious bacteria.

Bacteria Bloom – Also referred to as new tank syndrome. See nitrogen cycle.

Basking – An important procedure when a slider dries off and warms up. A RES will need an easily accessible area that is dry and approximately 10 degrees warmer than the water. This is beneficial as it helps prevent shell infections, allows the turtle to absorb UVA and UVB rays (if they are provided) and thermoregulate.

Bridge – A section of shell between the fore and hind limbs that connects the carapace and the plastron.

Brumate – Refer to hibernate for context.

Bullied – Refer to aggression for context.

Calcium – A critical element for healthy shell and bone development. It can be found in various vegetables, pellets and prey. It can also be offered as an additional supplement.

Carapace (top shell) – The dorsal, convex section of the shell that is divided into plates known as scutes.

Carnivore – The term for an animal that eats a diet consisting mainly of meat. Most RES have a preference for live prey and hatchlings may be only interested live prey.

Chelonia – The former term for Testudines, it can be used to refer to all turtles.

Chlorine – A chemical element used in water purification in municipal water supplies. It can irritate a turtle's eyes, respiratory system and membranes as well as destroy beneficial bacteria. Chlorine does evaporate within 24-48 hours or can be treated with a water conditioner.

Claws (Nails) – RES have sharp claws to rip apart prey and vegetation. Long nails are a sexual characteristic of male sliders.

Cloaca – A posterior opening on the underside of the tail that is the only opening to serve intestinal, urinary and reproduction purposes. The cloaca on a female is closer to the shell whereas a male's is further away due to the longer and thicker tail.

Clutch – Refers to a collection of eggs produced by a turtle in a single nest at a single time. A healthy, full-grown female might lay 3 or 4 clutches in a season and each may contain over twenty eggs.

Cuttlebone – A white, lightweight, chalky material that is made from the internal skeleton of the cuttlefish. Its calcium carbonate is used as a dietary supplement. It is inexpensive, easy to find and normally floats. Remove the hard backing and offer your turtle small bite-sized pieces to chew.

Death Zone – Temperatures that are too cool are often called a "death zone" since they are not cold enough for actual hibernation but cold enough to inhibit their metabolism.

Diurnal – A way to describe animals that are active during the day and rest at night.

Drowning – A serious situation in which a turtle has inhaled water and may be dead or appear dead. Illnesses, injuries, low water levels, decorations and equipment can cause this situation. Please refer to this section.

Dystocia – A term for an abnormal or difficult childbirth or labor. Refer to Egg Binding.

Ear Abscess – An ear infection that is easily noticeable in the form of a lump on either one or both sides of the head. Veterinary care is required.

Eggs – Female RES will produce eggs regardless if there is a male present. It is necessary to provide a nesting area to prevent egg retention or having them laid in water. Please refer to this section.

Egg Binding (Egg Retention) – Occurs when eggs are abnormally held within the body. These eggs can decay, deteriorate or become calcified. They become brittle and can cause an internal injury, bacterial infection, peritonitis and death. A suitable nesting area is needed but does not always prevent egg binding because stress, poor diet, age, illnesses, abnormalities and personality can be a factor. Please refer to this section.

Egg Tooth – A small, sharp protuberance on the beak of a hatchling. Its only function is to assist in the breaking out of the eggshell, which is known as pipping.

Fanning – An event in which a male RES will expose his penis. It occurs underwater and should retract itself. It is possible for it to get injured or bitten by another turtle.

Feeder Fish – Any fish that is bred to be used as live prey. Guppies and minnows are preferred choices while goldfish are fatty and more prone to carry disease and parasites.

Fertilizer – Refer to chemical contamination.

Filtration (Water) – A device that removes debris and impurities from water by means of a physical barrier (mechanical), chemical processes or biological process. A good, reliable water filter is absolutely necessary to maintain water quality.

GFCI – A ground fault circuit interrupter. A residual-current device disconnects a circuit whenever the flow of current is not balanced.

Gravid – A term that represents a female RES carrying eggs. When a female is gravid, she will need an appropriate nesting area so she can lay her eggs properly. A female RES can be gravid without the presence of a male and the eggs will not be fertilized.

Gut-Loaded – The process by which prey is raised and fed nutritious foods and supplements with the intention of passing those benefits to the animal when the prey is eaten.

Hard Water – Water that has a high mineral content, usually calcium and magnesium. It is generally not harmful to RES, though they may develop mineral deposits on their shells and on your tank equipment. Refer to water softener for treatment options.

Hatchling – Refers to newborn turtles or any other animal that emerges from hard-shell eggs. After one year, hatchlings can be referred to as yearlings.

Herbicide – Refer to chemical contamination.

Herpetology – The branch of zoology that studies reptiles and amphibians. Reptiles and amphibians are sometimes referred to as a "herp". When searching for veterinary care, make sure your provider is an experienced herp vet.

Hibernate – A state of regulated hypothermia. Reptiles are said to technically brumate or undergo brumation. This is a period of inactivity and lower metabolic rate.

Hyperthermia – A condition of having abnormally high body temperatures. This is a serious threat to the immediate health of a slider. Refer to POTZ for related info.

Hypothermia – A condition of having abnormally low body temperatures. This is a serious threat to the immediate health of a slider. Refer to POTZ for related info.

Hypocalcemia – A calcium deficiency in the bloodstream. This could lead to metabolic bone disease (MBD), also known as soft shell syndrome.

Impaction – A medical condition that occurs when a RES consumes something, usually gravel, that they cannot digest. Once it is ingested, it will block the digestive tract and can be fatal without immediate medical care.

Keratin - A fibrous protein that is the main structural element of a turtle's shell and beak. In people, it is the main element in hair and fingernails.

Lethargy – A general lack of activity or energy. Lethargy is usually a symptom of illness or incorrect habitat settings.

Neosporin – An antibiotic ointment that offers infection protection. It can be used on minor skin injuries and a turtle should be dry docked after application.

Nest – A female RES will carefully construct a nest where she can lay her eggs and shelter them. It will be perfectly concealed once she has completed her task. She must be allowed to make a proper nest or she could suffer from future medical problems.

Nitrate – A byproduct of the bacteria that break down nitrites. Nitrates should develop naturally once bacterial colonization is established.

Nitrite – A byproduct of the bacteria that break down ammonia. Nitrites should develop naturally once bacterial colonization is established.

Osteoderm - Refer to scute.

Oxalic Acid – Oxalic acid and oxalates are nephrotoxic acids that are present in some plants, which are known to block calcium absorption. They can bind and inhibit calcium and these types of plants should absolutely be avoided.

Oxygenated Water – Well-oxygenated water is needed for the nitrogen cycle and for hibernating turtles.

Oxytocin – A hormone that is administered by a vet induce egg laying in gravid females.

Pet Trade – Refers to the industry that relentlessly breeds millions of slider hatchlings a year. This industry also attempts to lobby the U.S. government to lift important safety regulation regarding turtle eggs and hatchlings.

pH – A measure of acidity or alkalinity in the water. The measure of the activity of hydrogen ions in a solution indicates this acidity. Pure water is neutral and has a rating of 7; tap water might be slightly alkaline and have a rating of 8. Slightly acidic water may inhibit bacterial and fungal growth.

Photoperiod – The length of daylight that should guide you to determine how long your turtle's lights should be on. Mimicking your seasonal photoperiod is physiologically beneficial while using a timer will make it easier for you. Lighting should be on for around 12 hours a day, depending on the time of year. Too little or much light will disrupt your turtle's activity and sleep cycles.

POTZ - (Abbr. Preferred optimal temperature zone.) The recommended water temperature for RES is between 75-78F (24-25.5C); basking temperatures should be 90F (32.2C). Having a correct POTZ will allow your turtle to thermoregulate. A POTZ is beneficial as it allows for proper digestion, growth, reproduction and metabolism. Temperatures that are too cool are often called a "death zone" since they are not cold enough for actual hibernation but cold enough to inhibit their metabolism.

Prefilter - As an attachment, a prefilter is an additional foam pad is added to a filter intake, providing additional mechanical filtration. A prefilter can also be used to add an extra layer of safety for small turtles placed with a powerful filter.

Preformed Pond – A type of readymade pond kit that is pre-molded. These can provide an attractive habitat for a turtle and could also be modified to work above ground and indoors.

Prey – Refers to any intentional and unintentional live food placed with your turtle. RES are natural predators and will instinctively go after live foods, even though they may show no initial interest.

Purine – Refer to gout for context.

Pyramiding – A long-term and sometimes permanent shell disfiguration. The various causes can be excessive feeding, irregular feeding, inadequate diet, poor habitat conditions and genetics.

Quarantine – The process of isolating a new turtle prior to its introduction to an existing turtle community. This period can be used to detect illness, infections, parasites and disease. It is recommended to quarantine for as long as 3 months.

Reverse-Osmosis (RO) – A water purification technique in which water travels through various semipermeable membranes.

SCL – (Abbr. Straight carapace length)

SCUD – (Abbr. Septicemic cutaneous ulcerative disease)

Scute (Osteoderm) – The bony external plates on the shell. The scutes in the carapace are as follows: nuchal scute, neural or vertebral or central scute, marginal scute and pygal or supracaudal scute.

Septicemia – A very serious medical condition, resulting from the immune response to a severe bacterial infection in the bloodstream. It is essentially blood poisoning, a serious and life-threatening infection that requires immediate emergency care.

Shedding (Shell, Scute) – A normal and expected occurrence with RES. They will shed over a period of time. Their appearance begins to lighten or become a golden color (due to an air pocket) and will eventually lift up. Old and injured scutes are the most likely candidates for shedding.

Shedding (Skin) – Shedding or molting of the skin is a normal occurrence with RES. Excessive shedding may be an indication of high water temperatures or fungal infections.

Shell Rot – Refer to Septicemic cutaneous ulcerative disease.

Soft Shell – Refer to metabolic bone disease.

Stock Tank – A water storage container that is used to provide drinking water for animals such as cattle or horses. These can be useful as alternative and inexpenisve indoor or outdoor housing for RES. There are several manufacturers who produce plastic tanks at various sizes. Rubbermaid manufactures a line of plastic stock tanks that are 50, 70, 100 and 300 gallons and can be found at farm supply stores.

Stomatitis – Refer to mouth rot.

Straight Carapace Length (SCL) – A method of measuring your turtle. To obtain this measurement, you stretch a line between the front of the shell and the back, ignoring the curvature of the carapace. It is best to use a rigid ruler as opposed to a tape measure.

Stress – Refers to physical and mental condition that captive RES are in. Hatchlings and newly acquired turtles are likely under a great deal of stress. Do not to underestimate the impact that stress can have on a turtle's health.

Submersible Water Heater – An electrical device used to heat water to a certain temperature and maintain that temperature. A good quality heater should be fully submersible, unbreakable and have an adjustable thermostat.

Substrate – The loose material that is used at the bottom of a tank. It can affect water chemistry, filtration, and the well being of the aquarium's inhabitants.

Supplement – The reference of addressing deficiencies in a turtle's diet with calcium and vitamins. A healthy and well-varied diet will require little supplementation.

Tail – A flexible appendage that contains the cloaca. A female tail is shorter than a male tail, which also houses his penis.

Temperature – The degree of heat measured and expressed as hotness or coldness. The two widespread scales used are Fahrenheit and Celsius (Centigrade). Most of the references in this site are relative to the Fahrenheit scale. The recommended water temperature for RES is between 75-78F (24-25.5C); basking temperatures should be 90F (32.2C). Temperature measurement is extremely important in turtle care. Many inexperienced keepers unfortunately guess or use approximations. Thermometers are accurate, inexpensive and there is no reason not to have a few.

Terrapin – In general, a turtle that is semi-aquatic. RES are terrapins because they spend time on land and at basking areas. Different cultures may refer to all turtles as terrapins. Terrarium - An enclosure simulating a relatively dry habitat. These may not be suited for RES habitats because they are not designed to hold large amounts of water.

Territorial – Confined in a small tank, RES can develop a protective and aggressive behavior within that space. They may flutter their paws or escalate a situation into biting. An increase in space does not guarantee less aggression, especially since a RES might feel the need to compete for food. While some RES spend a majority of their lives alone, they don't always adjust well to new tank additions.

Textured – A reference to the surface of a basking area. A dry, textured area allows for the plastron to dry off.

Thermometer - A simple and inexpensive device that measures temperature or temperature gradient. There is no reason to guess or estimate water temperatures, especially since it cannot be done accurately or consistently. Many inexperienced keepers unfortunately guess or use approximations.

Thermoregulation - To regulate body temperature and keep it within certain boundaries. Refer to POTZ for related info. Abnormally warm temperatures above a POTZ is hyperthermia, abnormally cold temperatures below a POTZ is hypothermia.

Thiamin – Vitamin B1. Known to metabolize carbohydrates. Refer to thiaminase for context.

Thiaminase – An enzyme that destroys Vitamin B1 (thiamin). Vegetables and prey high thiaminase enzymes would break down thiamin, resulting in a Vitamin B1 deficiency.

Tortoise - In general, a turtle that is land based. RES are terrapins because they spend time on land and at basking areas but other cultures may refer to all turtles as tortoises.

Trachemys Scripta Elegans - The current trinomial name (genus, species, subspecies) of the Red Ear Slider. RES were previously classified as Chrysemys scripta elegans.

UVA – Invisible rays that promote normal behavior such as activity, feeding and mating. UVA rays have UV wavelengths of 380–315 nm. Sunlight, incandescent bulbs and florescent UVB lamps are sources of UVA rays. Refer to more extensive information in the lighting section.

UVB - Invisible rays that stimulate the natural production of the vitamin D3. This vitamin is required for the metabolization of dietary calcium and together with the calcium, plays a role in the prevention of illnesses such as Metabolic Bone Disease. Sunlight, MVB and florescent UVB lamps are sources of UVB rays. UVB rays have UV wavelengths of 315–280 nm. Refer to more extensive information in the lighting section.

Veterinarian (Vet, Herp vet) – A person trained and qualified to treat diseased or injured animals. Most veterinarians are educated in cats and dogs – not "exotic" animals like reptiles. It is important to find a qualified and experienced vet who treats turtles. A specialist of this type would be referred to a herpetological veterinarian or a "herp vet". Refer to this section about searching for a vet.

Vitamin A (Deficiency) – Hypovitaminosis A. This type of deficiency may cause a turtle's eyes to be closed or swollen. Vegetables such as carrots or a supplement such as cod liver oil contain vitamin A.

Vitamin D3 (Deficiency) – A lack of UVB rays or D3 as a dietary supplement. Vitamin D3 aids in calcium absorption and is needed to prevent calcium deficiency disorders such as metabolic bone disease and various organ dysfunctions.

Vitamin D3 – A critical vitamin that aids in the metabolization of calcium. Vitamin D3 is naturally produced with exposure to natural or artificial UVB rays. It can also be offered as a dietary supplement, however it should be done so carefully to RES who are D3 deficient and under the guidance of veterinary care.

Vitamin K (Deficiency) – A deficiency that can disrupt intestinal bacteria and cause bleeding in the mouth.

Warmth – Refer to basking for context.

Water Softener – Softening is a process that exchanges the ions of the hardness minerals. Other ways to soften water is to add distilled or RO water. Filter media options include peat moss or a water-softening pillow.

Wet/Dry Filter – A filter designs whose underlying principle is to promote maximum nitrification by having the bio media rotate between being in water and exposed to air, therefore introducing more oxygen to the biological media.

Wild RES – A slider that is not under captivity. It is never recommended to take wild turtles captive unless they need medical attention or need to be relocated.

Yearling – A description used for a RES after the first year of life.

Yolk Sac – The residual yolk that remains on a hatchling once it has hatched. It should gradually be absorbed providing nourishment. A hatchling may not be interested in eating during this time.

Chapter One: Understanding Red Ear Slider Turtles

The Red Eared Slider Turtle is a strong, semi-aquatic turtle that gets its name from the wide reddish stripe behind its eyes. The underside of its chin is rounded with a V-shaped notched at the front of its jaw and is not flanked by cusps. Its feet are webbed and they are strong swimmers and impressive divers.

Its body is a dark olive green and has thin yellow bars and stripes on the carapace, or the top of its shell, as well as its face and legs. As the red eared slider matures the green coloration of the top shell becomes covered with black pigmentation making them almost appear black with no markings visible. This is especially true for males as the turtle's age.

The top shell, or carapace of the RES turtle is oval in shape, it is smooth to the feel and is flattened with a weak keel. The bottom part of the red eared slider shell, or the plastron, is predominantly yellow in color and bears a dark marking on the center of each of its scutes. It has webbed feet to help maneuver itself through water when it swims.

The average length of a red eared slider turtle is 5 to 8 inches with a rare record of 11.8 inches. The female has a much thicker tail and is visibly longer than its male counterpart. The cloacal entry of a male red eared slider is found beyond the edge of the carapace whilst the opening for the female is at the rear or found under the rear edge of the carapace. The claws of the males, sported longer and curved, are used in mating and courtship.

In its natural habitat of the wild, the red eared slider turtle will usually be seen on logs, rocks, and other surfaces as it basks. They do this because, like most reptiles, these turtles are cold blooded and rely heavily on outside sources for heat and warmth.

The red eared slider turtles appear to share similarities with the painted turtle due to the bright markings both turtle species sport. The top shell, or the carapace, of this RES turtle is higher domed in comparison to the Western Painted Turtle and has been noted to be weakly keeled.

The top three things a red eared slider turtle needs to thrive well would be temperate surroundings, a proper, balanced diet and clean tank water. The proper care for the RES turtle, as with other turtles, is a lot more complicated than what most people assume. A responsible adult should be the primary caregiver of the RES and should take up the responsibility for the RES upkeep and the cleaning of the confines of where it is housed. An adult hobbyist is to be responsible for feeding it and monitoring the turtle for any possible signs of illness to ensure a long healthy life.

Basic Red Ear Slider Turtle Information

The red eared slider, native from Illinois to the Gulf of Mexico, is commonly confused with the Western Painted Turtle because of similarities in size and coloration of carapace. To distinguish a red eared slider from a western painted turtle, look for the evidence of a higher domed carapace which is weakly keeled.

Traits to quickly distinguish the slider include yellow marginal scutes, a yellow colored plastron covered in darker, blotchy markings with a red ear mark found immediately behind the eye. It is to be noted though, that this ear marking is not always apparent in older turtles.

Male sliders are smaller in size as compared to female sliders, and they sport long claws on their front feet which are utilized during courtship and mating.

Summary of Red Ear Slider Turtle Facts

Basic Red Ear Slider Turtle Information

- **Scientific Name:** *Trachemys scripta elegans*
- **Breed:** *Emydidae*
- **Size:** 15 - 20 cm or 6 -8 inches; females are notably bigger in adulthood
- **Maximum Length:** can grow up to 12 inches
- **Shell Texture:** smooth
- **Colors:** Olive green with bright red stripes behind its eyes
- **Temperament:** relaxed but can snap and nip when agitated
- **Strangers:** skittish and guarded
- **Children:** strongly discouraged

- **Other Pets:** strongly discouraged; may be introduce to similar breed
- **Exercise Needs:** Swimming, Diving, Hunting Small Prey
- **Health Conditions:** pre – dispose to illnesses such as Swollen and Closed Eyes, Ear Abscesses, Parasites , Shell Rot, Respiratory Infection , Metabolic Bone Disease (MBD)
- **Lifespan:** can live up to 20 - 50+ years

Origin and Distribution

Belonging to the *Emydidae* family, the red eared slider turtle is also known by its scientific name *Chrysemys scripta elegans* (formerly *Trachemys scripta elegans*). In the US, the normal range of occurrence for this sort of turtle is from Illinois to the Gulf of Mexico and from the East Coast to western Texas.

Presumably due to people releasing pets, these turtles have also been spotted and found in other regions of the United States. This turtle likes to spend time in or around small bodies of slow moving water as well as ponds and marshes, which all supply many areas for basking as well as an abundance of food. However, the red ear slider turtle has also been spotted around lakes and rivers.

The red eared slider occupies and is found in the Mississippi Valley from Illinois to the Mexican Gulf. All occurrences of the red eared slider, as well as other pond sliders like the Cumberland slider and the Yellow-bellied slider, is attributed to intentional pet release or accidental escape from captivity.

The red eared slider has particularly been successful in establishing itself in the east, north and south of its original range in the United States. It is found in four states east of its natural range which include the states of California, Arizona, Hawaii and Oregon. It is also found in a state south of its native range in Florida. The eight states of the north of its natural range are West Virginia, Ohio, New Jersey, Kentucky, Michigan, Pennsylvania, Massachusetts and Maryland.

South Korea, Guam, Japan, Thailand, France, Germany, Israel, South Africa and Australia are other countries where red ear sliders have been introduced and it has spread out worldwide in other parts of Europe and Asia.

Species and Subspecies of the Red Ear Slider Turtle

Of the thirteen to nineteen pond slider subspecies, three are native to the United States. These three pond slider subspecies native to the US are the yellow-bellied slider

(*Trachemys scripta scripta*); the Cumberland slider (*Trachemys scripta troostii*), and the red-eared slider (*Trachemys scripta elegans*).

The range from southeastern Virginia to northern Florida is where the yellow-bellied slider calls home. Found in the upper portions of the Tennessee and Cumberland Rivers, from southeastern Kentucky and Virginia to northeastern Alabama is the Cumberland slider. And lastly, occupying the Mississippi Valley from Illinois to the Gulf of Mexico is the red eared slider turtle.

Several color changes are presently sported by the red eared slider turtle and is available in the specialist reptile trade because hobbyists have shown great interest in selective breeding for aesthetic appeal. The albino red eared slider, when in the juvenile stage, is stark lemon yellow in color with prominent patches of orange-red on the sides of its head. As these albinos mature, the yellow color fades into a cream-yellow hue.

Other morphs or color changes seen in the red eared slider are marketed under the category of "pastel" red eared turtles. This term, "pastel", is used for a range of varying color morphs of red eared sliders by different degrees of reduced black (hypomelanism), reduced yellow (hypoxanthism), digression in pattern as well as varying degrees of yellow and red pigmentation.

Defects, the expression of recessive genes, and asymmetries in many pastel sliders, suggest of inadequate temperatures or incubation. Reduced size of one or both eyes, unusual enlargement of one or both eyes, and asymmetry of shell pattern are some examples.

Red Ear Slider Turtle Environmental Issues

Red eared slider turtles were once the most sought after item in the pet trade with an estimated 5-10 million turtles exported all over the world. This fact is why sliders are called "dime store turtles". Sadly, due to unclean conditions and lack of know-how on turtle care and maintenance by pet store keepers, very few of these sorts survived long in captivity back then.

Owing to this decline in the past, turtle farms were soon established in the southeastern part of the United States, mostly in Mississippi and Louisiana to stave off the lowering numbers of the RES turtle in wild stocks. More than 150 turtle farms were in operation by 1960. Over 9,000 adult turtles were taken from the wild each year since then because the existing farms were not self-sufficient. This practice seriously depleted the natural population of the species in some areas. It was also these same farms who were responsible for capturing adult sliders with intent to export as food to Asian countries.

The US Food and Drug Administration banned (in the US and in Canada) the sale of turtles with a carapace length of 4 inches in 1975, because these turtles were found to be carriers and transmitters of the salmonellosis disease caused by Salmonella; this is a grave disease which affects the digestive tract and it had infected several thousands of children and was also the cause of the spike in deaths attributing to how children handled the turtles and proper after-handling sanitation.

Using various techniques and methods to limit the incidence of the spread of deadly Salmonella, the turtle pet trade industry has not slowed down in the export of a large numbers of hatchlings and adults to other countries. The frequent use of Gentamicin, an antibiotic, has resulted in the development of many antibiotic-resistant strains. Due to the continued export of pond sliders, a vital route for global spread of human salmonellosis had been identified.

Chapter Two: Things to Know Before Getting a Red Ear Slider Turtles

Raising and caring for a red eared slider successfully will require more than a rock at the bottom of a bowl of water. Red eared sliders, like most aquatic turtles will require more in terms of habitat, proper diet and lighting to live a healthy life. In this section you will learn about a few important points you need to consider before going out in search of a red eared slider turtle. Contrary to popular belief, red eared sliders require more work and effort on the part of a turtle hobbyist/caregiver. They tend to grow larger than what pet store owners and vendors imply, hence will need more room later as it grows. A large tank to accommodate its growth, special lighting for reptiles and a diet appropriate for the amphibian are just some of the things you will need to provide for the red eared slider turtle.

To increase your chances of bringing home a healthy red eared slider there will be a few things you will need to investigate. Scrutinize the shell, the eyes and the turtle's activity (or lack thereof) as well as how they swim. Witnessing the turtle in its present environment and seeing these turtle traits and its living conditions yourself will give you an idea of the turtle's health and well-being.

When a red eared slider is young, a small aquarium will suffice for the time being until it grows. As the red eared slider matures, it will require a roomier tank which can contain well over 50-100 gallons of water. Turtle owners have learnt to be creative and have used all kinds of housing ideas to provide spacious areas for their red eared slider; utilizing preformed pod liners to give the habitat of the turtle a pond-like appearance; fitting the turtle's tank with RES turtle friendly vegetation it can snack on and making sure lighting, temperature and water quality are all in check and conducive to the needs of the RES turtle.

Other owners, who choose to keep their RES outside in more "natural" conditions, double up on securing the safety of outdoor ponds the RES turtles live in by fencing the pond area - keeping the turtles in and possible predators out. You will want to think about putting the turtle outdoors for a minimum part of the year. You will want to network with experienced owners and hobbyists to determine how to set up an outdoor pond for the RES turtle.

No matter where the turtle is housed, clean water quality is to be maintained. Another habitat requirement not to be overlooked is the provisions of UVB, UVA lighting as well as supplemental heat. Setting up the all these can be a challenge at the onset but once set up, cleaning the RES turtle's aquarium can be kept to a minimum IF properly maintained.

Do You Need a License?

Selling turtles which are less than 4 inches long has been illegal in the United States since 1975 because they are susceptible to harboring salmonella on their skin. This law is still very much in effect and should be kept in mind.

While red eared sliders of any size can potentially carry the deadly Salmonella bacteria, the smaller, baby turtles are those usually chosen to be purchased on a whim and gifted to small children as pets. Refrain from gifting RES turtle's to little children who would mindlessly and naively handle these adorably cute turtles with little or no regard for proper sanitation after handling.

Individuals caught selling turtles violating the 4-inch rule could face being fined of up to $1000. However, if the turtles in question crossed state lines with a value exceeding $350, the crime is bumped up to a felony under the Lacey Act. Lacey Act violations can sum up to a whopping $250,000.00 in penalty fines or a sentence of 5 years behind bars. First time offenders are given a reprieve and will typically receive a fine of about $2000.00.

It is not legal to own a red eared slider turtle in the state of Massachusetts; instead, an owner of an existing pet slider will be grandfathered and the turtle may be allowed to be kept by a hobbyist for the rest of its life under the condition that the owner keep a clear date-stamped, in-focus photograph of its belly (plastron) as documentation. An existing red eared slider need not have a permit in MA but the state presently prohibits these as pets due to invasive occurrence.

Obtaining permits and licenses for the red eared slider turtle depends on the state or country of its occupancy. Be reminded though that it is illegal to release a red eared slider turtle to the wild in many American states. The distribution and selling of red eared slider turtles are restricted in many states unless the 4-inch turtle length rule is met.

How Many Red Ear Slider Turtles Should You Keep?

Before getting yourself into a situation which may later surprise or worse alarm you, you will want to find out how feasible it is to own more than one of these comical looking RES turtles.

Keep in mind that these tiny, little green cuties will grow to be very large and messy aquatic animals which will require you a lot of your attention and time. Not only will you have to consider the size it can grow to - a whopping 12 inches in some cases - you will also need to factor in the available space you have at home which may later be swamped with tanks and aquariums if you are not thoughtful.

A red eared slider which is well cared for in captivity can be expected to live for well over 20 years. There have been some which have been recorded to live up to 50 years old and beyond.

Keep in mind that it is illegal to release a red eared slider back to the wild and if an individual were caught they are going to be heavily fined. So if you become overwhelmed by a nest of red ear slider hatchlings, you will have to do what is right by researching and looking for ways to correctly disperse them.

Do Red Ear Slider Turtles Get Along With Other Pets?

The red eared slider is an amiable, even-tempered reptile able to share space with its kind and a few other turtle species given that they are provided enough room to be housed comfortably. Many hobbyists aim to integrate many of their reptile pets in one habitat and though this is possible and often successfully accomplished by zoo professionals, tanks housing mixed-species of turtles or reptiles can be very challenging to keep clean, is quite costly and will be time consuming.

Red - eared sliders although friendly toward most other turtles can become aggressive when its territory is threatened. It can display its innate voracity and prey upon smaller animals it is housed with if the mix is not thoughtfully researched and backed up by facts. It is best to do your homework now and determine which species would get along well with your RES turtle.

If you are setting to house multiple species in one tank you will need to follow a thought out strategy to help your efforts of to integrate them. First, you will need to provide lots and lots of extra space with many hiding places and visible barriers. Next, you will also have to make sure that all residents are fed separately to make sure that one is fed more than the rest. It will also be smart to break up the habitat with different hiding nooks with barriers in order for the submissive one of the lot to be able to escape facing the dominant animal should a new pet be introduced to pets already established.

How Much Does It Cost to Keep a Red Ear Slider Turtle?

Prices of turtles vary depending on its sort. The RES turtle is a relatively affordable pet, hence its wide popularity. The upside of getting a red ear slider turtle is that it can easily be obtained for as low as $20 in a pet store whilst some specific types can be bought from reptile breeders for a loftier price.

No matter the sort of turtle you have in mind, you will want to consider the availability of space in your home as these turtles can grow to be quite big as it matures. You may opt to search online to fid out of any RES turtles in your area being given up for adoption. There are also non-profit and rescue organizations to visit and consider before making a purchase and opt to rescue one instead.

In contrast to the affordable pricing of an RES turtle, maintaining one as well as housing it can set back a hobbyist an average of $ 800-$1000 at the onset. Expect to pay around $150-$250 for a suitably sized aquarium/terrarium for the turtle to live in with a tank of about four feet in length and no less which can contain 50-100 gallons of water. You will also need to consider and factor in equipment like UVA and UVB lighting, thermometers, a filtration system, a basking platform and a ramp leading into and out of the water for your semi-aquatic ward. All these additional fixtures and sundries can set a hobbyist back about $400.

Factor in the expense for water treatments to remove chemicals like chlorine since turtles pretty much "go" where they eat and water will need to be cleaned regularly to avoid the incidence of parasites, infections and shell rot. You will also want to factor in the yearly electricity costs of keeping an aquarium clean, tempered, lit and conditioned to the needs of the RES turtle.

A red eared slider will need minimal medical attention but it is strongly suggested that a new red eared slider be taken to the vet to make sure it is in the pink of health before it is brought home. Should a caregiver notice a shift in its appetite - outside of the normal given, when females are egg laden and have little to no appetite - the turtle will need to be brought to the vet immediately for a quick check up.

Turtles must be treated as every bit as an expensive pure bred puppy would be treated and a potential caregiver/hobbyist should be aware of the responsibilities of caring for one and must be ready to take on this charge with utter commitment.

What Are The Pros and Cons Of Keeping a Red Ear Slider Turtle?

As with other pets, cold blooded or warm, red eared sliders too have their advantages and disadvantages. Knowing the plus and minuses of acquiring one will not only allow you to ask yourself important questions of readiness and financial capabilities to care and raise one or more, it will also reveal information you should know to be able to gauge, measure and assess your patience, means, time and desire to share space and home with one, two or more of these chill out sun - baskers.

Pros for the Red Ear Slider Turtle

- Red eared slider turtles have a long life expectancy
- They are quiet "sun-worshipers" who love basking
- They are funny creatures who would seemingly beg for food from their caregiver

Cons for the Red Ear Slider Turtle

- The red ear slider is not permitted to be sold in most states and carry big fines if released into the wild haphazardly.
- It costs a lot of money to set up, equip and maintain its habitat.
- Time maintaining its habitat will be frequent and scheduled.
- It has been known to be a carrier of the bacteria Salmonella.
- Native to the southern United States and northern Mexico, the RES turtle has shown to establish itself in

many other parts of the world due to export, escape, and pet releases.

It has, in fact, become an invasive species in many places and has competed with the native species of the lands it has reached. The International Union for Conservation of Nature (IUCN) lists the red ear slider turtle amongst the 100 most invasive species.

Chapter Two: Things to Know Before Getting a Red Ear Slider Turtles

Chapter Three: Purchasing Your Red Ear Slider Turtle

Be reminded that selling RES turtles under 4-inches in length has been, and is still, illegal in most US states. You would want to practice responsible ownership and not promote the ill methods employed by other pet stores when acquiring these tiny basking creatures of both water and land.

Red eared slider turtles are also widely known as dime store turtles giving hint on the amount of money needed to purchase one. Sliders sold on streets should altogether be stricken from your go-to list. Buying from Internet pet sites is no better than going to a pet store since there is no assurance of humane methods of procedure whilst these turtles were produced and harvested.

An individual could purchase one from a pet store for as low as $20. The price goes a little higher when the turtle is obtained from a reputable reptile breeder. Something to remember is that many sliders sold by dealers were raised in turtle farms. However, they would most likely be able to provide records and would likely be the most informed of the turtles history since these were under their supervision when they hatch the eggs.

Inspecting the turtle's environment, where the turtles are up for purchase, is one way to tip off a potential buyer to issues with their upkeep that will have a big impact on the turtle's future health. Look out for overcrowding in tanks and dirty water which are the usual pair of signs that point to a negative environment. Watch and observe the turtles and determine if they are alert and active as well.

On Adopting Rescues

Adult red eared slider turtles are a common occurrence in pet shelters and rescue centers for a number of reasons. The turtle could have escaped its confines, an overwhelmed hobbyist may have bitten off more than they could chew and decided to let go of its ward, and a host of other reasons for why an adult slider is up for adoption.

Adopting from rescues is not only a good way to give a turtle a new lease in living loved and cared for, it also discourages the purchase of hatchlings from indiscriminate turtle breeders who are only out to make a quick buck. And a quick buck is what a red ear slider makes at $20 a head for a lot of about 5-30 hatchlings each birthing.

It is probably best to look for a rescue nearest your area to facilitate visiting and consultations. Here is a list of a few rescues to check out:

Phoenix Herp

<http://www.phoenixherp.com/how-we-help/surrender-a-pet.html>

Turtle Rescue New Zealand

<http://www.turtlerescue.co.nz/turtle-adoption-new-zealand>

Mid – Atlantic Turtle & Tortoise Society

<http://www.matts-turtles.org/red-eared-sliders.html>

Forgotten Friend

<http://forgottenfriend.org/sliders/>

Turtle Rescue League

<http://www.turtlerescueleague.com/pet-turtles/turtle-adoption>

Turtle Rescue of Long Island

<http://www.turtlerescues.com/red_eared_sliders.htm>

How to Choose a Reputable Red Ear Slider Turtle Breeder

It is quite challenging to identify a reputable reptile breeder from other breeders. Because of breeding methods varying from natural occurrence, red eared slider turtles have been developed to project color morphs unusual of the naturally bred sort.

These are common when turtles are bred in captivity. Most breeders today breed red eared sliders for pet lovers and reptile hobbyists. So it will still be largely up to the future turtle caregiver to research and seek out the best breeders who are open to answering questions about the origins of the turtle, the methods employed during production and hatch period. Allowing you a walk - through of their facilities to see the conditions and living environment of the animals housed within their site is another good indicator you want to determine; all these could indicate a breeder who aims to follow the protocol for breeding these turtles.

Stay away from discounted red eared slider turtle traders since the discount itself could be a giveaway of an abundance of turtles resulting to slashed prices in order to be rid of excess. Pet stores housing red eared sliders with other exotic animals from other countries is also to be avoided as the exotic animals could be carriers of diseases which could be passed on to the turtle.

Tips for Selecting a Healthy Red Ear Slider Turtle

Upon determining your financial capabilities as well as the determination to provide a red eared slider all the necessities it requires for a well - balanced existence, you will have to conduct a very simple physical exam of the turtle in question.

Red eared slider turtles are alert and inquisitive when healthy. They would immediately jump from their basking spot into nearby water when approached. Pick up the turtle and determine whether it weighs heavy or light. A light turtle many be ill. The next test is to gently tug at one of its legs. The reaction of an ill turtle will be slow and less vigorous whereas a healthy turtle will be quick to react strongly.

Scrutinize the top and bottom halves of its shell. They should be smooth, hard and sans dark or light spots and markings. A shell soft to the touch could indicate shell rot. Take note of the occurrence of open wounds which may require medical attention from a vet.

Chapter Four: Caring for Your Red Ear Slider Turtle

Your new red eared slider turtle will need specific requirements to be met to allow it a chance of living a good, long and happy life with you. Knowing more about what it takes to care for one, what entails after acquisition and what to expect at any stage of its life as it grows are information vital to the success of your new union.

Making sure that your red eared slider turtle is provided with a comfortable habitat that would promote its overall physical and mental wellness are just some of the little details important to know. Temperature regulation and atmosphere control is a vital part of your turtles need as it cannot regulate body temperature on its own. Knowing what temperature the turtle thrives in best equates to it being able to metabolize itself in an artificial setting.

A young RES should be kept warm with water temperatures ranging from 82-85 F, than the average healthy adult. Keeping temperatures low around 65 - 72 Fahrenheit will be reason for the turtles to stop eating and respiratory infections could result. If you reside in places where temperatures plummet below 75 degrees - whether indoors or out - it will be strongly advisable to fit the aquarium or pond with a heater.

You will need to regularly check and monitor the water temperature of the tank. As a rule, the wattage is to range between 3-5 watts for every gallon of water. Also avoid pre-heaters as this will not provide the accurate temperature for the RES turtle.

As with taking in any sort of pet, a good rule of thumb is to find out how ready you are in terms of taking on the sole responsibility of maintaining the turtle's environmental temperature as well as the regulation of heat in the water you provide for it to swim.

The Basics of Reptile Thermoregulation

To say that reptiles are cold-blooded animals is commonly heard but also a large misrepresentation of this fact. The question that should be asked instead is what temperature is deemed as cold and to what is this temperature compared to if deemed cold?

Cold blooded in its true definition means a reptile has no ability to warm up their bodies by themselves from the inside as we humans are able. The reptiles therefore will need to source the heat it needs for warmth from factors existing outside its body. This is the purpose of thermoregulation.

Thermoregulation is a vital part of a reptile's existence to help it maintain temperatures high enough for its physical metabolism to work well. Reptiles seek out this heat in various ways like sun basking or sitting on a warm rock when left in its natural environment.

Since reptiles are not equipped with the luxury of being able to regulate its body temperature itself, it is imperative to give it areas inside of its tank aquarium or enclosure a wide selection of temperature picks. Again, avoid pre-set heaters as this may cause more harm than good to the animal.

When in the wild a reptile will have available to it many temperature areas to select from according to the needs and wants of their bodies at any given time. However, in captivity the dynamics quickly shift and the reptile will be largely dependent on its caregiver/hobbyist to recreate an environment which will closely mimic the heat and warmth of temperature spots naturally occurring in nature depending on what they require at any given time.

The metabolism of a reptile is extremely poor when temperatures fall below 5 degrees Celsius and much higher temperatures are needed to aid in jobs like digesting food. The reverse of this scenario results in the same negative outcome when temperatures are too high to work its metabolism efficiently. Temperature also directly plays a big role in the different biological workings of the reptile and optimal temperature will likely be different for a variety of species.

It is for the reason that reptiles cannot regulate its own body temperature that thermoregulation is applied in order to create, for the RES turtle, an atmosphere closely resembling what it has otherwise missed if it were in its natural environment. Generally, the higher the temperature, the more efficient is reptile's metabolism. Whereas, temperatures sustained above 41 degrees Celsius is often times deadly to a great number of reptiles.

Red Ear Slider Turtle Housing or Enclosure

Providing habitation for a red eared slider turtle can be challenging at the onset of conception, design and execution. A hobbyist must consider a number of factors as it prepare a well suited environment for the new turtle pet.

The size of a turtle aquarium will depend on a number of considerations like the reptiles growth spurt, size of the reptile upon maturity, the area space it will need to thrive without anxiety or threat to its safety, as well as the possibility of sharing the space with other turtles or reptile species. These sun - baskers will require habitation closely resembling their natural environment which is warm and with deep enough water for them to dive and swim. This area should also have a dry and warm spot where they can lounge, bask in peace and for females, to lay hatchlings.

Choose a glass enclosure if feasible. Other less costly alternatives are acrylic, plastic tub, a wading pool or a tank. Take into consideration the size of an adult slider which can reach up to 12 inches in length, which will require a 55-

gallon aquarium at least for it to be able to do all it does as it naturally would in its natural surroundings.

The enclosure will need to be fitted with basking spots, a ramp to get in and out of water as well as an ample amount of hiding nooks to where it can retreat. Driftwood, cork bark or a platform of sooth, stable rocks can be used for basking areas. Sand can be used to recreate the shore of a beach. You may elevate this area a little with a piece of plexi - glass glued to the bottom of the tank.

Fit the aquarium with a tight-fitting mesh cover to prevent the turtle from wandering out of its enclosure and to protect the reptile from possible falling debris.

Temperature and Lighting Requirements

The air temperature in the general location of the aquarium must be kept at approximately 75 degrees Fahrenheit constantly. An infrared bulb may be used if the temperature in the general area of the aquarium is colder.

An incandescent bulb of 75 watts or lower will be sufficient for the turtles basking spot and will emit enough heat and warmth the turtle requires. The basking spot temperature should be an ideal 85-90 degrees Fahrenheit closest to the bulb. All bulbs must be firmly fixed to something sturdy outside of the terrarium and fastened securely above the screen cover to prevent falling and electrocution accidents.

An acrylic or glass housing should not be placed directly where the sun shines as this may get too warm.

Full spectrum ultraviolet (UVA and UVB) fluorescent lights must be utilized to complement the production of vitamin D-3 in the turtle whilst providing a habitat closely resembling its natural setting. Factor in the cost of bulbs as this will be a twice a year expense when replacement is needed because the efficiency of it emitting true full-spectrum will diminish over this period of time.

The light is to directly shine on the turtle and should NOT be filtered through plastic or glass. The use of a timer will be wise so the turtle follows a normal day-night cycle as it should.

Maintaining Humidity

The Red Eared Slider requires water to be at a 75 - 85 degree Fahrenheit. Keep in mind that the turtle is a cold-blooded animal unable to regulate body temperature on its own. Should temperatures plummet their metabolism will slow down and they will be rendered inactive if the water temperature becomes too cold which could also have a bad effect on their digestive systems resulting in health issues for the turtle.

A submersible water heater can be used to maintain the ideal temperature of the water, which should be on a thermostat. You will need an estimated 5 watts per gallon of water. Be certain that the thermometer is set below the water line and do not forget to switch this off when bailing water out of the tank. Follow the manufacturer's directions and guidelines to avoid electrocution.

Critical to the turtle's health is the quality of water in the tank. The water becomes a likely place for bacteria and other unwanted organisms to thrive due to uneaten food particles, feces and urine which contaminate the water. This will be a health hazard for your turtle and an unsightly scene for you to bear as a dirty tank will stink up the general area of its location. Clean the water regularly with a double filtration system. Depending on the size and design of the aquarium with consideration for the turtle's size in mind, an internal canister, an external canister or an under gravel filter can be used to do the job.

Regularly replace the water with fresh water making sure you achieve the proper habitat temperature of the tank before placing your turtle back inside. You will also want to use a de - chlorinating agent to treat the water before filling in the tank. Utilize a siphon to remove 25-50% of the water in the aquarium, using it like a vacuum to suck out the dirty liquid and dirt particles trapped on the aquarium bed.

The whole aquarium must be drained, cleaned and refilled with filtered, de - chlorinated water every 1 to 2 months depending on the aquarium conditions. Do not ever attempt to manually start the siphoning process with your mouth. You will not only gain a mouthful of funk and gunk, you would have also exposed yourself to a host unwanted, sickening bacteria.

Feeding your turtle outside of the tank in a separate feeding tank saves you a great deal of work by minimizing the incidence of food particles in the water, should this be your choice of feeding method the water will need to be replaced once a week at a minimum.

Think of adding aquatic plants to your turtle's habitat. Not only will it make the aquarium look livelier, the aquarium plants will also be perfect hiding nooks and a good source of turtle snack and could possibly assist in removing and minimizing waste from the water. Think about using an air stone to help water circulation and provide better filtration.

Chapter Five: Meeting Your Red Ear Slider Turtle's Nutritional Needs

Aside from providing it a safe haven where it can grow without obstructions or limits, the red eared slider turtle will require a balanced diet as well for it to thrive successfully under the care of a responsible hobbyist/caregiver. Red eared slider turtles must be given a variety of animal and plant based foods in order to ensure a well - balanced diet. Baby red eared slider turtles must consume more protein from animals and is hence its meals should be started off based on such.

It is sound to offer a young red eared slider turtle some vegetation in its diet whilst it is young - giving it this option at this early stage doesn't ensure it will consume it, but at the very least, it will be less likely to refuse greens as it matures. As the red eared slider matures its taste for food shifts to a more herbivorous diet and as this shift happens, vegetation is to make up a significant portion of the adult red ear slider's diet.

The Nutritional Needs of Red Ear Slider Turtles

Young red eared sliders are primarily carnivores who later turn out to become adult omnivores. The diet of this turtle sort must be balanced with the inclusion of meat-based protein sources as well as fresh vegetation. Any potential hobbyist should not solely rely on commercial diets. Juveniles need to be fed daily and as the turtle grows into adulthood this frequency is lessened to once every other day.

Containing a good combination of vitamins and minerals, commercial pellets are beneficial to a red eared slider's diet because it is fairly nutritious - not to mention convenient. But as convenient as pellet food can be, it is still advisable to offer your turtle a wide selection of fresh foods which will provide a wide range of nutrients in various forms and can be absorbed by the turtle better if given in the natural state.

Offering live food choices is also more stimulating to the red eared slider turtle and is a good way to enrich its health as well as opportunity to hone its innate hunting abilities. As a rule of thumb, limit pellet feeding to about 25% of its diet and make up for the rest of its nutritional needs with items listed in the following section of this chapter.

Animal or high-protein foods

A large composition of your turtle's diet should comprise of meal worms, shrimp, bloodworms, crickets, aquatic snails, krill, wax worms, silkworms and earthworms. Larger turtles can be given bigger prey like feeder fish or tadpoles. Do this in moderation as many experts have warned of feeder fish possibly carrying parasites whilst other fish (like goldfish) are too fatty in composition to be used to feed the turtle on a regular basis.

The threat of pesticide is a real one and can be dangerous if the prey caught is contaminated with

dangerous chemicals. Visit your local bait shop or pet store
and find out how prey is harvested and collected. Pesticides
pose dangers to the turtle which may lead to suffering from
intestinal parasites. The same is true for vegetable and
vegetation randomly collected outdoors. You will also want
to make sure that the greens you provide your turtle is toxin
and pesticide-free.

Avoid giving your turtle frozen fish or give it
sparingly. There are some fish that when frozen increases
the levels of an enzyme in it which obliterates vitamin B1
making the food useless in terms of nutritional value.

Lean beef or cooked chicken do not offer a balanced
nutrition for the turtle and is also cause for the tank or pond
water to quickly foul. Should you opt to feed your turtle
these foods, do it occasionally as a treat and consider feeding
these to the turtle outside its tank. Remember that
moderation is essential whenever feeding the red eared
slider turtle any foods outside of its natural staple - too
much protein from chicken or beef can contribute to the
turtle developing liver disease.

An absolute no is to be said if the matter of raw
feeding a red ear slider is the question. The risk of bacterial

contamination to you and the turtle is a very real threat and should altogether be nixed.

Plant-based food, including fruits and vegetables

Commercially bought turtle pellets can provide a sufficient base diet for the red ear slider but this should be supplemented with a diversity of other foods to meet its overall nutritional requirements.

Greens and vegetation are to make up the other part of the red eared slider turtle's diet. Offer it vegetables in the form of mustard greens, collard greens, dandelion greens, bok choy and kale. Keep iceberg lettuce off its diet as it has very little nutrition. On the other hand, dark green lettuces, like romaine lettuce, should be given sparingly.

A potential red eared slider turtle caregiver can opt to put aquatic plants in the aquarium or pond which the turtle would usually favor to snack. Plants like the submerged anacharis are often to its liking as with water lettuce, duckweed, azolla or fairy moss, frog-bit and water hyacinth. Other acceptable vegetable to add to its diet would be carrots, green beans and squash.

There are a number of experts and seasoned red eared slider turtle caregivers who swear by giving the turtle a selection of fruits such as melons, apples, bananas and berries. It is to be noted, however, that these aren't part of the natural staple of the red ear slider and may cause it to develop diarrhea. Should you choose to give your red ear slider fruit, remember to keep the portions minimal and in limited frequency.

Important Vitamins and Minerals

Look for a good reptile multivitamin which contain a sufficient amount of calcium and vitamin D3. The supplementary vitamins are to be combined with the food it is given at least a couple of times a week.

Another good way of giving it additional calcium is placing a cuttlebone in its tank. A cuttlebone can usually be found in the bird section of any pet store. Just affix the cuttlebone to the tank with the use of suction cup clips, or just have it float in the water.

A high ratio calcium-mineral supplement containing Vitamin D-3 should be given with each meal. This can be done by dusting the food the turtle is fed with this much needed supplement. These vitamin supplements are recommended to be given at least twice a week.

Tips for Feeding Your Red Ear Slider Turtle

Caregivers of amphibians, especially the red eared slider, through time and experimentation have discovered a few basic practices to follow which ensure a clean enclosure as well as easy clean up. All these sum up to an overall healthy turtle in a healthy environment.

To maintain a cleaner tank, you may want to opt to feed your turtle outside of its tank to minimize clean up after feedings. This may sound a little tedious to do, but it will save a potential caregiver the hassle of having to tidy up after every turtle meal. The fact is feeding the turtle outside of the tank keeps the quality of water cleaner in the long run. This not only saves you from replacing the water more frequently than you should, it also works best for the turtle, helping avoid shell problems, ear and eye infections, etc.

Overfeeding will promote obesity in the red eared slider and will garner an excess in waste matter that a caregiver will need to remove. Be careful about over feeding your RES.

Chapter Six: Red Ear Slider Turtle Care and Husbandry

Understanding the normal behavior of a red eared slider can assist a potential caregiver in giving it optimal care. Figuring out its natural behavior and determining that the red eared slider is at liberty to carry out activities necessary for its well-being, such as swimming or basking, are things a caregiver should be aware of to secure its overall health and wellness.

Amongst the most common culprits of red eared slider health problems are improper diet and incorrect environmental conditions. Lack of required needs for warmth can lead to diseases like metabolic bone disease (MBD) as well as vitamin A deficiency.

Knowing what to provide a captive red eared slider turtle is essential to its quality of life and all around well - being. A potential hobbyist, with all intents of raising one, must be aware of how to care for and what to provide a RES for it to be a happy camper and a content silent buddy who not only loves rays hitting all the right spots, it also has this amusing trait of begging for food when hungry. Be careful you don't get suckered into feeding the turtle more than it needs. In terms of feeding your turtle, more isn't always better.

Understanding Red Ear Slider Turtle Behavior

Red eared sliders are cold-blooded animals that are unable to regulate body temperature by itself. It is largely dependent on sun rays to keep its body temperature at a level which allows it to function properly. Because of this the Red Eared Slider is commonly seem basking under the sun and soaking up the rays as a matter of survival and comfort. It is not unusual to see sliders sitting atop each other as they share a basking spot with their kind or other sorts of semi-aquatic turtles.

These sliders have weak hearing but makes up for this auditory deficiency through feel and vibrations, making them very alert even when they appear to have nodded off whilst basking.

They quickly retreat into the safety of the water when threatened or when they feel any sort of impending danger to themselves. Clinging to submerged tree limbs, sliders will sleep underwater during the night. It is also not unusual to see a slider floating on the surface of water with the aid of their inflated throats.

Around October as temperatures falls to 10 degrees Celsius, turtles begins to brumate. Many of these turtles spend this season of inactivity submerged and resting underwater but they have also been found under hallow stumps and shallow banks.

These turtles do not brumate in groups and prefer to find a spot for them to spend this period of tranquility. Brumation can be interrupted by warm spells between January and February, when they could become active for a short time, surfacing to hydrate and feed. But as the temperature drops back down, so will the RES turtle commence its brumation period. The turtle makes a permanent appearance signaling the end of brumation around early March to late April.

Red Ear Slider Turtle Hibernation or Brumation

Reptiles like the red eared slider turtle do not hibernate but in fact, brumate. This period of brumation is signified by less turtle activity save for the occasional surfacing for water and food. Red ear sliders can be found in brumation at the bottom of ponds or shallow lakes over the winter season. It is usually around October, when temperatures fall below 10 degrees Celsius, that red eared sliders are less active.

The Red Eared Slider is a semi-aquatic turtle which can safely brumate indoors or outdoors if conditions are safe and given that the water it is in does not freeze. If the turtle is kept in a pond outdoors, it will manage and respond to changes and shifts in temperature as well as the length of sunlight and it will know instinctively when to ready itself to brumate.

An animal living in a tank indoors will need artificial stimulation with the aide of its caregiver in order for these changes to come about. You should consult with your vet, check local pet clubs for information and ask experienced hobbyists if you are unsure of this period or if you are not confident of recognizing signs the turtle may display of its readiness.

The red eared slider is a semi-aquatic turtle whose sex is determined by the temperature it is in during a specific period of its existence. It is also a reptile whose breeding success hinge on periods of brumation. Feed your turtle a correct amount of vitamin A before its fasting period during winter. You will want to up its meals with foods rich in vitamin A such as carrots, squash, kale, broccoli, collard greens, dandelions, alfalfa, sweet potatoes, cantaloupe and peaches.

You will also want to increase its fiber intake and include timothy hay and alfalfa. Should your pet already have these present in its normal diet then just feed your pet as you usually would. You will need to fast the turtle 2 - 6 weeks before its brumation to make sure it has no undigested food in its system. Brumating a turtle a month after it had last eaten could die. Brumation should instead be delayed to avoid undigested food to decay and cause fatal bacterial infections.

The caregiver is to reduce the photoperiod in the turtle's tank a little at a time over a period of time. The turtle is then put on fast for 10 days to ensure its bowels are empty. During the last 3 days of fasting the slider is to be soaked in water to make absolute certain that it has emptied its bowels of all contents.

Most turtles brumate from 2 - 4 months. Other species brumate for up to 6 months but it should be noted that this length of time is not required; to shake off uncertainty consult with your vet.

Preparing a Hibernaculum

Cold-blooded creatures such as reptiles go through a period of brumation during winter. This is a time of limited activity. Knowing the proper equipment to fit a terrarium with is essential to a healthy environment and a healthy red eared slider.

Turtles in captivity need not brumate to thrive or survive. However annual brumation periods increase its odds for successful breeding. Preparing a hibernaculum for your turtle will require you to do extensive research for you to know the specific requirements of your turtle ward.

Your red eared slider turtle originates from the US and Mexico, therefore it is not like tropical turtles, which have no need to brumate. Unlike their tropical counterparts, these turtles will need to brumate under the proper conditions. They will also need to mate, hatch, grow and live in conducive, temperature controlled environments.

You will need to purchase an aquarium large enough to hold - and its eventual adult size - and house red eared slider hatchlings. You may start off with a 10 gallon tank but a 20 gallon tank is strongly advisable as you will soon realize that your turtle will outgrow a small one very quickly.

In addition to the tank, a caregiver will also need to provide the turtle with a full-spectrum UVA and UVB lighting fixtures, a basking light, a dry basking area and a water heater.

There are some red eared sliders which are able to thrive year round in an outdoor pond. But even outdoor ponds need to be large enough to house the turtle, under controlled and temperate conditions. There is also the matter of safety of the turtle from predators, pesticides and cold spells.

Chapter Seven: Red Ear Slider Turtle Handling and Temperament

Always check with your vet, a seasoned caregiver or a reputable reptile breeder of the basic needs of your new red eared slider turtle. Your research into knowing more about the RES and what it needs to thrive in health is vital to its overall wellbeing. These turtles can be exciting to have around and may find you wanting to play and handle them when time permits. Handling this animal safely is one of the most important care tips for both handler and turtle. Read on to find out more about the temperament and proper handling of the RES turtle.

Red Ear Slider Turtle Temperament

It may take about a week or so for you and your new turtle to get acquainted on a more personal, face to face basis. The Slider turtle is a small animal used to finding itself as prey to a few larger, much hungrier animals, therefore it is not unusual for this turtle to duck and cover when it feels the least bit of threat to its being.

Once integrated to its new surroundings and as soon as it warms up to your person this funny little green-shelled being will happily acknowledge your presence and may even show its excitement by swimming up and down it's little own pond. It would bob its head in apparent approval when it sees you walk into the room. Be mindful of your fingers as a RES turtle may snap and nip at your fingers if handled too soon or incorrectly.

Tips for Handling your Red Ear Slider Turtle

During the early stages whilst making a decision of whether or not raising a red ear slider is for you, a responsible hobbyist will want to arm himself with vitally important details on how to handle this turtle sort safely. It is a well-known fact that particular kinds of reptiles, as well as certain amphibians, have a tendency to be Salmonella carriers, these are bacteria which causes infections in humans. The red eared slider is one of those reptiles which transport and transmit the dreaded disease.

Little children, toddlers, babies and young tots are never to be left alone with a red eared slider because toddlers have a penchant for exploring with their mouths. Anyone who handles a red eared slider is to wash their hands and wash them well after handling the animal. This goes for adults and most especially little children. An ounce of prevention is better than a pound of cure - not washing after handling a red eared slider could cause the handler to get sick.

Avoid handling your new red eared slider turtle for at least a week after getting it. Allow it to get used to its new surroundings and let it inspect everything you have painstakingly done to make its new home a warm and welcoming one. Give each other time to get used to one another - your turtle will get used to you being in its presence when you feed it and gawk at it from the other side of its tank.

Once used to your presence, it will equate your being there with feeding time and will start to acknowledge you as it bob its head in seeming approval. It may even swim excitedly to and fro as you come closer to its tank. When you and your turtle have had enough time to get to know each other from behind its enclosure, you might now want to say hi on a more personal level. When you do decide to pick up your turtle, do so gently so as not to give it a fright.

To do this, grasp your turtle like a burger making sure to securely but gently hold on the sides of its shell from the center of its body. Make certain that you have a firm but gentle grip on your new buddy because you don't want turtle slippage to happen if it suddenly moves its wet and slippery body.

Excessive struggling and a display of stress are signs your turtle isn't quite ready to be handled yet. Limit this period to shorter meetings and build up the length of bonding time as the turtle learns to get used to these periodic social visits.

The Growth and Development of Red Ear Slider Turtles

Nature in all its wondrous marvel has a way of giving us humans cues and signs for situations, instances, and events of which a potential caregiver should be aware. Learn more about the growth and development of the red eared slider turtle and empower yourself with useful knowledge to successfully care for one.

A pivotal phase of embryogenesis conforming to the incubation temperature determines the gender of the turtle. Most reptiles are temperature-dependent and lack sex chromosomes which dictate gender. When incubated at temperatures ranging between 22 and 27 degrees Celsius, pond slider eggs will become only males. Incubated at a much warmer temperatures, eggs in this condition will only come out female.

When baby sliders are ready to meet the world, they hatch out of and emerge from the egg looking much like tiny adult red eared sliders.

Behavioral Characteristics of Red Ear Slider Turtles

Whether in its natural surroundings and environment or housed in a tank or a makeshift pond, red eared slider turtles have been observed to actually enjoy the company of others like it. They are often seen in groups basking together, one on top of another either on fallen trees and broken logs usually near a small body of water.

They are social creatures and like to hang around with their own kind whenever possible. They may not be big in talking, given that they have not been heard to make any particular or distinguishing sound, but they do in fact communicate with each other through touch and vibrations.

Basking in groups is not only an opportunity to socialize this activity also offers the security of safety in numbers, as well as much needed sun exposure which helps stave off the occurrence of parasites on their shells.

They are watchful of predators who may want to make them the main course of the day - specially steering clear of otters, mink, foxes, raccoons as well as most medium-sized beasts which prey on them and their eggs - by taking refuge in nearby water. They are also able to quickly retract their heads and legs and hide inside their hard shell should it get the whiff of danger. Consider the genders of the turtles you are thinking of housing together. A male RES is very territorial and may fight and bully other smaller turtles for basking space.

A male and a female RES placed together in a shared enclosure can cause stress and anxiety to the female during mating season and they may need to be separated. Multiple species sharing space can be tricky as a red eared slider may outgrow and out compete other turtle species since it is grows large and strong and they are much more driven than cooters, map turtles and painted turtles. Consider housing multiple species in a large outdoor environment where they can best thrive.

These turtles go into brumation sometime in October when temperatures are relatively low. They are usually out of land sight and are at the bottom of shallow lakes and ponds only coming up for occasional feeding and hydration.

Chapter Eight: Breeding Your Red Ear Slider Turtle

This turtle sort would, in the wild, generally begin to breed after two weeks of brumation in order for its babies to hatch when the weather is comfortably warm and conducive. Breeding red eared sliders is a lot more challenging than many people presume. Putting a male and female in the same space isn't enough to ensure successful breeding. A caregiver will need to take pains in mimicking the turtle's natural environmental conditions and life cycle as closely as they possibly can for positive results.

It is not recommended for red eared slider turtles to be casually bred. There is a method to successful red eared slider turtle breeding which includes a period of brumation. Brumation increases the likelihood of breeding success for the turtles. The season of breeding for red ear slider turtles last from late spring to early summer. The courtship dance and mating activities of this turtle sort usually happens between the months of March and July and all of this happens underwater.

Once brumation is completed and the turtles have once again taken in food and has enough stored energy is the perfect time to pair off males and females. Place the male and female turtles together in a tank and allow them about 45 minutes to breed. If nothing happens, separate the two turtles and try again in a couple of days. You will know that breeding has begun when the male has mounted the female with both their tails entwined.

A nesting area is to be provided for an egg-laying female. Do this by housing the female turtle in a gestation tank of 20 gallons with 4 inches of loose potting soil like vermiculite for the female to lay its eggs in. Make sure that the female turtle is kept warm and damp, disturbing her as little as possible during this period.

Do not be alarmed if you notice her skipping meals or completely ignoring food as this is perfectly natural for an expectant female red eared slider turtle. In an ideal situation for laying eggs the female will lay its eggs in two months. The hatchlings, under ideal conditions will take about 80-85 days to hatch.

Neglect to provide the female red eared slider turtle a nesting space should most likely result in an egg bound turtle, which is a very serious condition the female could suffer. To increase the chances of successful breeding, the caregiver will want to fashion a hibernaculum using a large tank. The tank should have an inch-thick of potting soil with some loose hay, soil and moss. The temperature of the tank is to be regulated and slowly dropped to about 50-55 degrees Fahrenheit to make the hibernaculum a conducive surrounding for brumation.

Begin reducing the photoperiod on the turtle's lights little by little over a period of time and put the turtle on fast for a span of 10 days. Soak the slider during the last 3 days of fasting to make certain it totally empties its digestive tract.

The next thing you will want to do is to place your red eared slider in a hibernaculum - this is a tank with an inch thick of potting soil with some loose hay sphagnum, moss and soil. Artificially drop the temperature slowly within the tank until it is about 50-55 degrees Fahrenheit.

Selection and Care of the Breeding Pair

Red eared sliders are easier to mate when they reach sexual maturity. A higher success rate is noted when turtles undergo brumation. The sexual maturity of a female is between 5 - 7 years and a male is around 2 - 4 years.

After brumation, a potential breeder is to slowly raise the temperature in the turtle's habitat for over a period of two days until temperature in the tank reaches 85 degrees Fahrenheit. This is the best time to start natural mating selection.

Place your male and female turtles in a shared space. If the timing is accurate then the male should start courtship of the female by impressing it with its mating dance. The female will then show acceptance or rejection of the male's advances either by being receptive to, or if unfavorable, fighting off the male.

Laying and Care of the Eggs

Many caregivers do not realize they have female red eared sliders until the turtle begins to lay eggs. It is noteworthy to remember that females, in the absence of a male red eared slider, will lay infertile eggs. Provide the female a nesting area which consists of potted soil and moss, cover it with some hay where the temperature is suitable for the female to start laying its eggs.

Although a female red eared slider will drop their eggs in the water, this is not how the red eared slider prefers to lay its eggs. The reason why it is important to provide a nesting area for a female is because some of these females would rather keep or retain their eggs than to lay or drop them in water. The female turtle will then be facing a serious problem of becoming egg bound.

Female turtles, being amniotes, are required to nest on land. These females show preference for soft, sandy soil with the nest site located in an area well exposed to the sun. Nests are created with the female digging on the soft soil with its hind legs, not far and usually 200 meters of water. The female makes a nest which is no deeper than 10 to 12 centimeters and here it will lay 2 to 30 soft, oval shaped eggs. These eggs, as they are being laid and buried in the sand are fertilized as well.

Caring for the Hatchlings

After a few months of the breeding process, the hatchlings would have arrived. Once they do, do not disturb, touch or move them for about a day. Observe in silence instead as the hatchlings. If the hatchlings do not feel secure they will not leave their shell. When they have all dug out of the soil you may start transferring them to their own tank. The ideal number of hatchlings per tank is 12 hatchlings per 20 gallon tank.

Provide the tank with a full spectrum light that mimics the rays of the sun and proper heating with temperature ranging from 80-85 degrees Fahrenheit. You can find all the necessary equipment at most pet stores.

Chop up appropriate food, like pellets, earthworms or mealworms, to feed it making sure that the portions are small enough to fit their tiny mouths. You may try offering the hatchlings lean beef or ham if they refuse to eat. Alternatively, you may employ a dropper to force-feed a dropper full of turtle vitamins and beef blood to those who refuse to eat. You only want to do this to whet their appetites until they eat on their own, so do not overdo this procedure. Keep in mind that deciding to incubate red eared slider eggs is a lot more difficult to do on your own and is not recommended or encouraged unless the hobbyist/caregiver is aptly prepared and experienced as a breeder.

Chapter Nine: Keeping Your Red Ear Slider Turtle Healthy

Take heed that everything needed to treat a reptile illness costs much more, eats up a significant amount of time and is sadly not as successful as when treating a similar human malady. There are also limited drugs and even more limited treatments available for a sick reptile. Being that reptiles have notably lower metabolisms compared to humans, it takes longer for them to display progress and even longer for them to start to heal. In addition to these, there are very few learned reptile vets and you would have more than sufficient reason to dedicate a portion of your energy and time to practicing prevention.

Turtles, in its natural environment, are prey to many larger animals. Predators can zero in on a sick animal. Showing any signs of weakness or vulnerability increases the chances of a smaller reptile being another animal's dinner. Therefore it is not in a turtle's best interest to display indications of illness. A reptile in captivity is usually assumed to be in the pink of health until it is within a couple of hours away from its death. This reptile would have been ill for an undetermined length of time but because signs were so well hidden no one was the wiser.

Keeping your red eared slider healthy means it is utterly vital that the animal is checked in on every single day. That its behavior is keenly observed every day, noting any changes in its manners or routine, and lastly that its habitat and all equipment helping to smoothly operate the turtles tempered domain is checked on a daily basis.

This may sound like a load of work but the secret to doing an effective job is in the quality of effort you put into the task. It will take your diligence and discipline to make a habit out of these tasks until they become a routine in your everyday doings.

Mentally ticking off the same things as you watch out for the same indicators every time, and doing them at the same time each day will soon come naturally. A good time to carry out this routine health and safety check is during feeding time when you can observe each one for any unusual changes.

Common Conditions Affecting Red Ear Slider Turtles

When faced with some common health issues which affect the RES turtle, it is strongly advised that the RES turtle be put in quarantine and isolated from other pets until it is given a clean bill of health.

This measure prevents the spread of whatever illness your RES turtle may be experiencing. There are clues and signs a hobbyist/caregiver need to recognize and watch out for to catch any RES ailment before it becomes serious. Remember that with reptiles, there isn't much treatment to go around and even if there were, the results of treatment take quite a while to show progress. The best rule of thumb for any reptile hobbyist is to live by the saying "an ounce of prevention is better than a pound of cure".
You primarily want to keep the RES turtle's habitat clean, well lit, and temperate.

Notice that the enclosure you've taken great pains to set up outfit and rig to serve as a safe haven and an environment fit for happy turtle living is also the same exact enclosure which if left unmanned, unsanitary and unkempt becomes breeding ground for fungi and bacteria which can cause horrible medical conditions for the red eared slider turtle.

Remember to keep a red eared slider turtle's enclosure clean to ensure its overall health and wellness. Along with water quality, a responsible hobbyist should make certain that temperatures of the air, water and tank within its enclosure are regulated to assist the metabolism of the reptile as well as encourage an atmosphere of wellness.

Proper lighting will not only keep the turtle happy and warm; turtles also depend on these UVB and UVA lights to assist in the supply of much needed vitamins important in maintaining a tough exterior. Heat and lighting also helps to determine the sex/gender of the turtle (if you are taking care of females with hatchlings).

Should you notice any unusual signs or recognize symptoms of illness in the turtle, the first thing you will want to do is to remove the turtle from its usual enclosure and temporarily house it in another, much smaller, tank. Fill the temporary tank, with de - chlorinated water, to only a depth that submerges the lower half of the RES turtle's body making sure not to go higher past the carapace.

At this time, you will want to clean out its tank completely, making sure to clean each piece of furnishing, and equipment that goes into the habitat. You will also want to observe your ailing RES turtle and nurse it back to health from its temporary tank as you keep in touch, consult and discuss the situation with your trusted vet.

Swollen and Closed Eyes

One of the more preventable and easily treatable illnesses observed in a turtle is the swollen and closed eyes syndrome. This condition is largely due to improper lighting, hygiene and diet. This is almost always caused by a lack of vitamin A and vitamin D, both of which the turtle can get from a proper diet and proper lighting of its habitat.

Ear Abscesses

This usually occurs because of stagnant, rancid water and inappropriate lighting in the enclosure. Take your turtle to the vet and have the vet examine the slider should this be noticed. Clean out the turtles tank whilst putting it in quarantine in the temporarily tank where it can rest and heal. Take extra measure and make sure that the water, air and enclosure temperatures are just as the turtle would require. Make sure that the turtle is better before you deem it proper to move it back into its enclosure.

Parasites

Parasites and worms find their way into a red eared slider turtle's tank in a number of ways. Stagnant water can attract mosquito larvae and spoilt food from feeding the turtle in its tank can be some reasons. You will want to remove the RES turtle from the tank and clean out the tank and all its fixtures and fittings to make sure there are no left over, hidden larvae in crannies and hidden nooks.

Soap out the whole tank, scrub down and dry out all fittings and fixtures before allowing them all to dry. Make sure that you have scrubbed all the corners of the tank clean with soapy water before wiping it down with paper towels.

While working on the clean - up of the aquarium, bring your RES turtle to the vet for a quick visit/check up to make sure that it is not infested with worms and if this should be the case, to give it the proper treatment it needs before returning it to its aquarium. Make sure that the turtle is treated and well, and the tank clean and filled with clean, de - chlorinated water before putting it back into its tank. Making sure the infected turtle is better and that the tank is clean staves off any future incidents and gives a little bit of guarantee that the incident won't worsen or spread and can be avoided in the future.

Shell Rot

If your red eared slider displays signs of soft spots, fluid beneath the surface of its plates, oozing pus or discharge, foul smell, shell plates falling off and exposing skin tissue, your turtle has shell rot. You will need to investigate its habitat for the root cause of the fungal or bacterial infection.

Too much moisture or too little of it, improper diet, improper heating or lighting and unsanitary conditions are either one or all to blame for shell rot. A turtles shell could also have been scratched, punctured or damaged by a sharp object in the tank so check that you remove any sharp edged objects inside the enclosure and that the whole tank has been cleaned sanitized, filled with de - chlorinated water, kept at the required temperature fit for the turtles needs, complete with proper lighting and appropriate heat before moving back the recovered red eared slider.

Respiratory Infection

Labored breathing, wheezing sounds and bubbles from the nose are all indications of a respiratory problem and merit an immediate visit to the vet. Congestion throws off the usually graceful swimmer and it may have a lopsided stride as it cuts through the water. The problem with reptiles is that they can't cough so they can't expel fluid. Fluid buildup in the lungs can be life threatening.

Metabolic Bone Disease (MBD)

Improper diet and lack of calcium are some of the culprits of this turtle condition. The lack or absence of UVA and UVB lighting can cause the turtles shell to slowly degenerate, deteriorate and soften.

Being that the brain needs calcium to function, if a RES turtle lacks the appropriate amount of calcium in its diet, the brain of the turtle will leech the calcium it needs from the RES bones which in the long run will weaken its structure and make its bones soft, eventually leading up to its brain ceasing function. When left unnoticed and untreated, MBD is a 100% fatal.

Preventing Your Turtle from Becoming a Health Hazard

In the event of inability to further care for a red eared slider, rid yourself of any ideas of letting the turtle back into the wild. Be reminded that a law against releasing a red eared slider indiscriminately back into the wild is illegal in most states in the U.S. Practice proper hygiene and wash your hands after you've handled the red eared slider. The slider is a transporter of the bacteria Salmonella which causes severe diarrhea in humans.

Do let a toddler play with the turtle without supervision and even with supervision it is best that the turtle and toddler get to know each other from the safety of a barrier separating them. A toddler may attempt to kiss a "too cute" red eared slider and come into contact with the very harmful Salmonella bacteria. Should a toddler, who is just as curious about the turtle as the turtle is to it, or a child manage to get hold of the turtle, calmly ask for the turtle and set it gently back into its enclosure and assist the child or toddler to scrub their hands clean.

Red Ear Slider Turtle Care Sheet

     Below is a quick summary of Red Ear Slider turtle so that you can quickly get the info you may need. It is a ready-reference guide for those wishing to locate specific information about this kind of turtle without having to read through the rest of this book, and it also allows you to easily refresh yourself about pertinent Red Ear Slider info that you may need at a moment's notice. For those still trying to decide whether or not a is Red Ear Slider the right turtle pet for them, this section allows them a quick peek into this amazing creature and what caring for one would entail.

1.) Basic Red Ear Slider Turtle Information

- **Scientific Name:** *Trachemys scripta elegans*
- **Breed:** *Emydidae*
- **Size:** 15 - 20 cm or 6 -8 inches; females are notably bigger
- in adulthood
- **Maximum Length:** can grow up to 12 inches
- **Shell Texture:** smooth
- **Colors:** Olive green with bright red stripes behind its eyes
- **Temperament:** relaxed but can snap and nip when
- agitated
- **Strangers:** skittish and guarded
- **Children:** strongly discouraged
- **Other Pets:** strongly discouraged; may be introduce to   similar breed
- **Exercise Needs:** Swimming, Diving, Hunting Small Prey
- **Health Conditions:** pre – dispose to illnesses such as Swollen and Closed Eyes, Ear Abscesses, Parasites , Shell Rot, Respiratory Infection , Metabolic Bone Disease (MBD)
- **Lifespan:** can live up to 20 - 50+ years

2.) Habitat Requirements

- 50-100 gallon tank / aquarium
- Sand, moss, soil, hay
- UVB - UVA lighting fixtures
- 50 watt bulbs
- Underwater Thermometer
- Fan
- Filtration System
- Siphon
- Fixtures and accessories for aquarium
- Water Heater
- Thermostat Regulator
- Mesh Wire Cover

3.) Nutritional Needs

- **Nutritional Needs**: Protein, Vegetables, calcium, Phosphorous, vitamin D3, Vitamin A; primary diet consists of 50% protein sources and 50% vegetable sources
- **Feeding Frequency (Adult):** Every other day or 2 - 3 times per week
- **Feeding Frequency (Juvenile):** Everyday
- **Water:** Should be freely available at all times

4.) Breeding Information

- **Mating period:** March to June (in the wild); year-round for turtles in captivity
- **Sexual Maturity (female):** 5-7 years (in the wild)
- **Sexual Maturity (male):** 2-4 years
- **Breeding Age (female):** 7 years
- **Breeding Age (male):** 4 years
- **Breeding Season:** between the months of March to June (for turtles in the wild); possible year-round mating for turtles in captivity.
- **Pregnancy:** about 60 days
- **Hatchling size:** about 3 - 30 hatchlings
- **Birth Interval:** birthed and laid by female
- **Hatchling size:** 1 inch in diameter

INDEX

F

G

H

I

J

L

M

N

O

P

R

Photo Credits

Page 1 Photo by user varunkul01 via Pixabay.com,

https://pixabay.com/en/turtle-amphibian-red-eared-slider-
   2292331/

Page 23 Photo by user Filio via Pixabay.com,

https://pixabay.com/en/turtle-red-eared-slider-water-turtle-
   1305879/

Page 33 Photo by user allyartist via Pixabay.com,

https://pixabay.com/en/red-eared-turtle-reptile-aquatic-
1488378/

Page 45 Photo by user Zoosnow via Pixabay.com,

https://pixabay.com/en/red-eared-slider-turtle-turtle-
   1762242/

Page 52 Photo by user raymondhal via Pixabay.com,

https://pixabay.com/en/turtle-red-eared-slider-green-690022/

Page 62 Photo by user Sergey_m via Pixabay.com,

https://pixabay.com/en/tortoise-amphibians-980000/

Page 70 Photo by user raymondhal via Pixabay.com,

https://pixabay.com/en/turtle-red-eared-slider-green-690806/

Page 77 Photo by user varunkul01 via Pixabay.com,

https://pixabay.com/en/turtle-amphibian-red-eared-slider-2292314/

Page 85 Photo by user JamesDeMers via Pixabay.com,
https://pixabay.com/en/turtles-red-eared-slider-amphibious-204710/

Page 93 Photo by user Filio via Pixabay.com,

https://pixabay.com/en/turtles-red-eared-slider-reptile-1305880/

Page 103 Photo by user JamesDeMers via Pixabay.com,

https://pixabay.com/en/baby-turtle-small-turtle-1456686/

References

Breeding Red Eared Sliders – Readerslider.com

<http://www.redearedslider.net/breeding-red-eared-sliders-advanced/>

Glossary – Readerslider.com

<http://www.redearslider.com/glossary.html>

How Much Do Turtles Cost – Petmd.com

<http://www.petmd.com/reptile/care/evr_rp_how-much-do-turtles-cost>

How to Handle a Red Eared Slider – Second-Opinion-Doc.com

<http://www.second-opinion-doc.com/how-to-handle-a-red-eared-slider.html>

How to Know If a Water Turtle Is Mating

<http://animals.mom.me/water-turtle-mating-10721.html>

Painted Turtle vs Red – Eared Slider – Nature Mapping Foundation Organization

<http://naturemappingfoundation.org/natmap/facts/painted_turtle_vs_red-eared_slider.html>

Red-eared slider
<https://en.wikipedia.org/wiki/Red-eared_slider>

Red-eared slider Care Sheet
<http://www.austinsturtlepage.com/Care/caresheet-red_ear_slider.htm>

Red-eared Slider Care & Feeding: Housing, Diet, and Characteristics – PetEducation.com
<http://www.peteducation.com/article.cfm?c=17+1797&aid=2613>
Reproduction: Mating

<http://www.redearslider.com/reproduction.html>

Thermoregulation – Pilbarapythons.com

<http://www.pilbarapythons.com/thermoregulation.htm>

The Biogeography of the Red-Eared Slider (Trachemys scripta elegans) - San Francisco State University Department of Geography
<http://online.sfsu.edu/bholzman/courses/Fall01%20projects/reslider.htm>

Treating common illnesses of the Red Eared Slider – WetWebMedia.com

<http://www.wetwebmedia.com/fwsubwebindex/treating%20RES%20Dis%20DarrelB.htm>

Feeding Baby
Cynthia Cherry
978-1941070000

Axolotl
Lolly Brown
978-0989658430

Dysautonomia, POTS
Syndrome
Frederick Earlstein
978-0989658485

Degenerative Disc
Disease Explained
Frederick Earlstein
978-0989658485

Sinusitis, Hay Fever,
Allergic Rhinitis Explained
Frederick Earlstein
978-1941070024

Wicca
Riley Star
978-1941070130

Zombie Apocalypse
Rex Cutty
978-1941070154

Capybara
Lolly Brown
978-1941070062

Eels As Pets
Lolly Brown
978-1941070167

Scabies and Lice Explained
Frederick Earlstein
978-1941070017

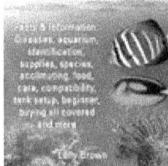

Saltwater Fish As Pets
Lolly Brown
978-0989658461

Torticollis Explained
Frederick Earlstein
978-1941070055

Kennel Cough
Lolly Brown
978-0989658409

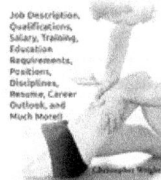

Physiotherapist, Physical
Therapist
Christopher Wright
978-0989658492

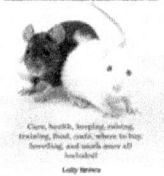

Rats, Mice, and Dormice
As Pets
Lolly Brown
978-1941070079

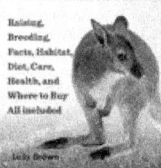

Wallaby and Wallaroo Care
Lolly Brown
978-1941070031

Bodybuilding Supplements
Explained
Jon Shelton
978-1941070239

Demonology
Riley Star
978-19401070314

Pigeon Racing
Lolly Brown
978-1941070307

Dwarf Hamster
Lolly Brown
978-1941070390

Cryptozoology
Rex Cutty
978-1941070406

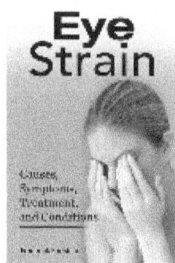

Eye Strain
Frederick Earlstein
978-1941070369

Inez The Miniature Elephant
Asher Ray
978-1941070353

Vampire Apocalypse
Rex Cutty
978-1941070321